PERSUASION

The Key to Seduce the Universe!

Become a Master of Manipulation, Influence & Mind Control!

Robert Moore

Table of Contents

Introduction

Even before mankind developed the amazing ability to communicate with the sophisticated verbal techniques we now use on a daily basis, the power to persuade others was of great importance and determined the way in which we were perceived and classed by our own species. Of course in those days persuasion was largely physical and it was generally the most powerful of our ancestors who came to be the dominant members of their various collective groupings.

Fortunately, we have evolved somewhat from those early prehistoric days and most of us are now able to rely on verbal and intellectual means as opposed to pure physical violence when trying to persuade others to follow a course we would like them to. That ability to persuade others is, however, still as important as it ever was and the more effective we are at using our persuasive skills the further we will get in achieving our own goals. Part of our persuasive ability is inherited and intuitive but so great is its importance that it has now been studied as a science for over sixty years. The fact that we are born with the ability to persuade others is demonstrated very clearly in children when we see their ability to cajole and coax their parents into doing what they want them to. As they grow they will develop a more complex array of strategies and it is those strategies that will, to a very large extent, determine how they progress in life.

Eric Knowles, professor emeritus of psychology at the University of Arkansas in Fayetteville explained it very clearly when he said "Persuasion is a basic form of social interaction. It is the way we build consensus and a common purpose."

Persuasion is used in social, political, business and religious environments and its mastery is crucial to each of us, even though we may use it in different ways. This book will look at the basic techniques of persuasion and how best to increase you own use of it, as well as techniques to protect yourself from being persuaded to do things you might not want to do. It is not a guide to coercion which though similar in the short term, will not produce the same results over an extended period of time. The aim is to teach you how to get people to want to do what you want them to and not to force them to do what you want them to. The difference may sound small but it is crucial.

Let's start!

Chapter 1

The Basic Techniques of Persuasion

Firstly, it is important to understand that there is a vast difference between persuasion and manipulation. It is perfectly possible to manipulate people into doing something they may not want to do but in the long term they will resent you for this and the result may well reduce your ability to persuade that person at a later date. A classic example of this comes from pressure selling techniques where customers are coerced into buying a product or service that they don't really want or need. The retention level of both the sales and customers drops off considerably and accounts for the bad reputation that some salesmen acquire.

Ideally persuasion is most effective when it leads a person toward something that both you and he want even if the final outcome may mean you getting something of more benefit to yourself than he does. The fact that you have both benefitted, even if not in equal amounts, means that the source of resentment is removed.

In this chapter we will look at some of the basic techniques which you will need to understand if you are going to become more effective at persuading others. In the following chapter we will look at some of these techniques in more depth.

1. Manipulation and Persuasion are NOT the Same Thing

Too many people confuse these and you must learn that they are completely different. Manipulation is the act of coercing a person to do something that they do not want to do through the use of force Persuasion, on the other hand, is an art. It is the art of getting a person to do something that benefits you but s also of great benefit to them and is in their own best interests

2. Persuade Only Those Who Can Be Persuaded

We can all be persuaded at one time or another, provided the timing is right and the context. However, for some people, it can take a lot of persuading. Take a look at the politicians and their campaigns – they focus their money and their time almost exclusively on the small percentage of voters whom are responsible for determining the outcome of an election. The very first step to successful persuasion is to identify and focus on the people who can, at that moment in time, be persuaded to follow you and your point of view. By doing this, a certain percentage of others, those who can't be persuaded at that moment in time, will be persuaded later on to change their course.

3.   Get Your Timing and Content Right

These are the building blocks of persuasion. Context is what provides a standard for what is and isn't acceptable, for example, an experiment carried out on Stanford prisoners showed that students who overachieve could easily be molded into prison guards with a dictatorial nature. The timing is what dictates what we are looking for from other people and from life. Often, when we marry, it is to someone very different to whom we may have been dating in our younger years, simply because, what we want at any given time is subject to change.

4.   Uninterested People Cannot Be Persuaded

You simply can't persuade a person to do something if the genuinely are not interested in what you have to say. In general, the human race is concerned primarily with their own individual selves and most of their time is spent thinking about three things – health, love and money. The very first step to persuading someone is to learn to talk to that person about themselves. Do that, and you have their attention. Continuing doing it and you will hold their attention for long enough to persuade them.

5.   Reciprocity is Compelling

Whether we like it or not, most of the time that someone does something for you, you feel innately compelled to return the favor. It's the way we are made, a survival instinct that goes back many millions of years. You can use that reciprocity to your advantage by giving someone something they want – you can then ask for something much more valuable back form them and they will feel compelled to do it

6.   Be Persistent

But not overbearing If you are prepared to keep on asking for what you want, to continue demonstrating real value, you will ultimately succeed in the art of persuasion. Take a wander back through history and look at the vast numbers of figures who have persuaded people through persistence, in both message and endeavor. Look at Abraham Lincoln, look at what he lost – three sons, is mother, his girlfriend, one of his sisters. He failed abysmally in business and he also lost at no less than 8 elections. Still his persistence paid off when he was finally elected as President of the Unties States. He never gave up and neither should you.

7.   Be Sincere in Your Compliments

Whether we admit it or not, compliments do have a positive effect on us and we are much more likely to place our trust in a person who is sincere and who makes us feel good. Try it – be sincere when you compliment a person, pay them compliments for something that they truly wouldn't expect it for. It's quite easy when you know how to do it and it costs nothing. The rewards will speak for themselves.

8.   Set Your Expectations

One of the biggest parts to persuasion is learning to manage the expectations of others when it comes to placing trust in you and your judgment. If a CEO was to promise his employees a pay increase of 20% and then give them 30%, he would be rewarded much more than the CEO who promised 20% and only delivered 10%. Learn to understand what other people expect of you and then over deliver on it.

9.   Never Assume

This is a bad mistake to make; to assume what people are looking for. Instead, offer them your value. Take the sales world; often products and services are held back because it is assumed that people simply don't have the money to purchase them or they have no interest in them. Be bold, get out there and say what you have to offer, say what you can do for them and leave the choice to them. Be persistent and it will pay off.

10.   Make Things Scarce

Virtually everything has a value these days, on a relative scale. We need the bare necessities to survive so they have a far higher value than something we don't need. Often we want something because someone else it. If you want to persuade people to want what you are offering, the best way to do it is to create a scarcity – the less there is, the more people want it.

11. Create a Sense of Urgency

One of the finer points of persuasion is being able to instill such a sense of urgency in people that they simply have to act straight away or miss out. If a person doesn't have any real motivation to want something now, they aren't likely to want it later on down the line either Its down to you to persuade them that time is running out; persuade them now or lose them forever.

12. Images are Important

Most people respond better to something they can see. Quite simply if they can see it, then its real, if you just talk about it then it might not even exist. Images are potent and pictures really do speak a thousand words. You don't actually have to use images, just learn how to paint that image in a person's mind.

13. Truth-Tell

Sometimes, hard though it may be, the easiest way to persuade a person to trust you is to tell them something that no one else will tell them, something about themselves. Facing up to the truth is often the most meaningful thing any of us will go through. Do it without any judgment and without an agenda and you will be surprised at how quickly that person responds favorably to you.

14.   Build Up a Rapport

The human race is a funny thing. We tend to like those who are more like us and this often goes way beyond the conscious into the unconscious. By "copying" or matching your behaviors, in terms of cadence, body language, patterns of language etc. you will find that it is easier to build up a rapport with them and easier to persuade them to your way of thinking.

15.   Be Flexible in Your Behavior

Have you considered why children are often so much more persuasive than adults are? It's because they are quite happy to work their way through a whole list of behaviors to get what they want – crying, being charming, pleading, trying to strike bargains, etc. Parent are stuck with just one response – No – which often turns to another – Yes. The more different behaviors you have in your repertoire, the more likely you are to be persuasive.

16.   Transfer Your Energy

There are those who drain us of our energy and there are those who fill us with energy. To be the most persuasive you have to be full of energy and you have to know how to transfer that energy to others. You have to be able to infuse them, motivate them and leave them feeling invigorated. It may be a simple case of eye contact, a physical touch or showing excitement in their responses o it may be something a little harder to do. Aster it and the world is your oyster.

17.   Clear Communication is Vital

If a younger child cannot gap your concept in a way that they can easily communicate to others, then it is simply too complicated. You have to simplify things, break it down into easy to understand bites and communicate it as clear as crystal. If people don't understand your message, you have no hope of persuading them.

18.   Be Prepared

When you begin your attempt to persuade people, it is important that you start from a position of knowing – knowing more than they do about themselves and their surrounding situations. Do your preparation properly and it will be to your advantage.

19.   Be Detached and Calm

If you are in a situation where emotion is running high, you will always be the most persuasive person if you are calm, show little to no emotion and remain detached from   the situation. In times of conflict, people will turn to you for help and they will trust you to lead them in the right direction

20.   Use Anger in the Right Way

Most people really don't like conflict and if you are prepared to escalate a situation to level of high tension and conflict, man of your adversaries will back down Don't make a habit of doing this and never do it when you are in an emotional state or are on the verge of losing control. Do use anger in the right way to gain the advantage.

21.   Be Confident, Be Certain

The most intoxicating quality, the most compelling quality is certainty. If you are confident and full of certainty, you will have the edge in persuading people to follow you. Believe in what you do, believe in what you say and you will always be able to persuade the next person to do what is right for them and to benefit you a well.

Chapter 2

How to Develop These Techniques

Empathy

Empathy is an important skill not only in regard to being persuasive but also in improving how we interact with people on a day to day basis. By learning to place ourselves in another person's shoes we not only become more sensitive to their needs and concerns but we also open the door to a more healthy and fulfilled life. Learning to actively listen is one of the greatest steps we can take toward showing empathy and developing a deeper understanding of another person and their concerns. It is that deeper understanding that will enable us to be more persuasive when we need to be.

Actively listening involves not only hearing what a person has to say but also requires us to be seen to be doing so. Looking a person in the eye and not becoming distracted by anything but what they are telling us is crucial. Once they have finished you should paraphrase what they were saying to demonstrate that you were paying attention and then you should articulate your own emotions to what they have just said. This will help them to regulate their own responses. Finally, you should indicate how your response makes you feel so that they too can understand you. Your perspective may differ from theirs and it is not necessary to just mirror their feelings. If you logically and eloquently demonstrate a different view point but remain sympathetic to theirs then you may provoke them into considering things differently.

We are all most interested in ourselves and there is a great tendency toward expressing our own views when we have a conversation with someone. We need to be aware of this tendency and to rein it in. In establishing empathy, it is vital that we do more listening than talking as our goal at this stage is to understand the other party and to make them know that they have been heard and understood. Even if their views are alien to your own the fact that have you have taken the time and effort to hear what they are saying will open doors toward you being able to persuade them in another direction. It is extremely frustrating when a person with a different opinion rides rough shot over those of our own. Once they have heard and understand what we have to say then we become less frustrated and more relaxed and this makes us less defensive our position.

Only when we have heard what they have to say and fully understood their position should we give a reply and we must make sure that reply is not too judgmental. To come on as judgmental at this stage is a sure way to close any doors toward offering some alternative and therefore persuading them to your point of view.

Credibility

It is all very well listening to someone else and getting a deeper understanding of what makes them tick but if they come away convinced that theirs is the only valid opinion you have not achieved very much. It is at this point that it is important that you establish your own credibility. The very word credibility stems from the Latin word credos which means I believe. Credibility is the feeling of trust and respect that you inspire in others. It may well take time to establish and is not always something that happens quickly. It can easily be lost however so guard it preciously.

You need to identify your core values and hold to them. Do not be afraid to draw lines in the sand and say these are points I will go to but will not cross. You also need to be authentic as the average person is far greater at detecting a false persona we may generate than we may at first suspect. Honesty is a non negotiable in terms of generating credibility.

It is important to understand whatever subject it is that you are anxious to persuade someone of and to become an expert in that area. Once you have done that you need to be able to communicate your expertise without seeming arrogant.

Remember nobody likes a smart arise. One way to do this is to include the person you are talking to and to ask for his input into the subject even if you already are aware of whatever information it is that he or she is presenting you with.

Communication is part of the process of establishing your credibility. This is a subject where practice and discipline pay dividends. You may not feel that you are good at articulating your opinions but don't accept that as the way you are. Like so many other skills, this is one area that really will develop as you use it. Concentrate on expressing yourself clearly and succinctly in all your communications and it will pay dividends when you need to persuade others. Also, when articulating you try to remain as unemotional as possible as being overemotional tends to weaken our communication skills. Finally try to always remain transparent. We don't trust people who are not open and that we feel are trying to hide something. It is not necessary to wear your heart on your sleeve but be honest about who you are and what it is that you believe. Even if people do not agree with you they will still develop a sense of respect for you as a person who is prepared to hold their position.

Similarity

In searching out those areas we have in common with others we create a path along which we can have a free flow of conversation and communication that are so important in order for us to persuade them of something at a later stage. These areas may be as diverse as the love of a particular sport to having children of a similar age. What the similarity is does not really matter. What is important is that we look for it and then use it as means to break down barriers between us. On a larger scale it may be areas of commonality in our objectives or goals even when we see the means of achieving them as being different. Research has shown that in face to face meetings women are far more adept at finding commonality than men as there is less competitiveness in the way they relate to one another. Men need to be aware of this and resist portraying themselves as too competitive.

We need to be intentional about finding similarities. Look on them as doors to other people's emotions and trust. Once we find them we can work on opening them and thus put ourselves in a stronger position in terms of persuading them. One method is to lead with your own interest and passions and see if that elicits any sort of shared ground. Be careful however that you don't then allow yourself to go on a rant in which you are the one doing all the talking and none of the listening just because the subject is one that you feel strongly about. Giving voice to your own feelings and opinions is not the main objective here. They were only being used as the key to getting the other person to communicate with you. Ask leading questions and then use your listening skills remembering that the most interesting people we deal with are the ones that are the best listeners.

If leading with your own interests does not reveal any similarities, then switch to asking questions. Where do you live? Do you have kids? Etcetera. If at first you don't get any where don't become too forceful and risk turning the conversation into an interrogation. It normally takes three meetings before common ground and trust are established. If your meeting is more at the corporate level, then make sure you have plenty of information at your finger tips. Google the company in question in advance and try to find out as much as you can about their goals and objectives before any meeting takes place.

Reciprocity

Reciprocity can be defined as the mutual or cooperative interchange of favors or privileges. In other words, if I do something for you then you will do something for me. This might at first sound like quite a mercenary motivation but it is so widely used in our society that we often don't even know that has happened. Remember the last time you were at a restaurant and you called for the tab? When it came it was accompanied by a nice little chocolate. Do you think they gave that to you for no reason? Of course not. What they hoped is that it would encourage a feeling of gratitude that might just lead you to coming back again at another time or, at least, that you might leave a bigger tip.

Research shows that when people give away free samples or tasters in super markets they increase their sales. This is because in giving something away they supplier generated a feeling that he was owed something and that the person who received the item in question would then be more disposed to purchasing that product.

It need not be something tangible that we give. Within a corporate environment if we give a compliment to a colleague's work or share recognition when complimented for a joint project, we also give. Likewise, in a relationship if we pay our partner a compliment as to how they look we are giving. The repayment may be something as simple as a more conducive and friendly atmosphere. The point is, the very act of giving has generated a response that is beneficial to us. Of course if your giving is perceived as being to gain a benefit in return then you create suspicion and distrust and your sincerity is immediately called in to question which can set you further back than you were in the first place.

Context and Timing

It is difficult to overestimate how important you timing is in terms of persuading people. There are times when a person will not respond to even your most persuasive arguments or gifts and it is always best to assess the timing before entering into any attempt to be persuasive.

Your wife enters the room in her curlers wearing the old dressing gown she inherited from her granny. You are feeling a little amorous and so you compliment her on how attractive she looks. Bad move. Immediately she will detect an ulterior motive and your chances of sleeping on the couch that night go through the roof. Instead you may try offering to run her a hot bath and bring her a cup of tea. You probably won't get where you were hoping to but at least you get to sleep in your own bed that night and you have not raised her suspicions to the levels that you would have with the false compliments. You are now in a position where you have not closed doors and have the opportunity to try another approach at a later stage.

Similarly, when you want one of your work colleagues to support you in presenting a difficult proposal at a meeting: it might not be a good idea to try eliciting his or her support just after he they received news that their much hoped for pay rise got turned down. In both these examples it would be best to take a step back for a second or two and observe. Once you are sure the other person is receptive to persuasion then it is time to make your move.

Interest and Need

To talk someone into buying something they neither need nor want may seem like a bit of a coup in marketing terms. It does however leave the seller in a sole winner position and this can only have short term benefits. There needs to be a win win scenario in any form of persuasion otherwise a feeling of manipulation will develop that normally leads to distrust and loss of credibility.

I may also be able to persuade somebody that he should do something that is solely in my own interest but inevitably at some point that person is going to recognize there is no gain for them and then they are likely to retreat from any commitment they may have made. This may well leave me in a more difficult position than I was in in the first place. It is therefore in my own interest to discover what the other person's needs and interests are and to incorporate those into my own strategic planning. As I mentioned earlier, joint interests may not be totally equal but there still needs to be interest or advantage to both parties in any negotiation that takes place if the other party is to be persuaded to act with me.

Scarcity

The perceived value of an item, be it a product or a concept, increases as its availability decreases. That unavailability may only be imaginary but it still needs to be perceived in order to exist. This immediately increases the value of the concept or item. I may be trying to persuade a client that a gem stone I have is of exceptional value. If he knows that that particular type of stone can be picked up along the beach where he lives it is highly unlikely I will be able to persuade him it has any specific value. However, if I persuade him that this is a very rare and is an unlikely to be seen again opportunity to purchase a gem of which there are very few others then suddenly he becomes more persuadable.

From a slightly different angle, if I see a beautiful girl in a bar and attempt to persuade her to come out with me, I am unlikely to meet with much success if there are dozens of other better looking men equally keen to woo her. If I can persuade her that I have some unique quality that makes me totally different to any of her other suitors, then suddenly I increase my interest factor and therefore my intrinsic value.

Persistence

Finally, there are times when sheer persistence is what makes the difference in whether or not you are able to be persuasive. In the example of the beautiful girl above it may be that my first attempts at getting a date simply meet with no success. Despite my best efforts to persuade her that I am in some way unique she may still turn me down. At this stage I have a choice. I can give up, accept that I have failed and sink into depression or I can try a different approach, perhaps at a time when she is more amenable to my advances. This takes us back to the subject of timing and of course it is assumed that I did not simply strut off in a huff after my first rebuttal, thus closing future doors.

In business terms you make a presentation to a client and it gets turned down at the first step. Keeping the doors of communication wide open and friendly means you may have a second opportunity. Hopefully you have learned something from your first failure and are able to correct that when you get a second opportunity. It is worth remembering that though somebody else may have been more persuasive than you at the initial presentation he may not have had the correct attitude of ability to follow up with what he proposed. If his proposal did not match up with his abilities he will have lost his credibility and provided you have kept doors to that client open by remaining polite and friendly, then the field is now more wide open for you than it ever was in the past. Even if the original project never comes your way again you have created a medium of communication through which your persistence might pay off at a future date.

Chapter 3
Influence

Unless you live alone on a desert island then the chances are that at some point, or points, in your life you are the member of a social circle in which you will have those whom you influence and those whom you are influenced by. The more influence you control the better your powers of persuasion will be as it is the people highest up the influence chain that tend to be the most persuasive.

For starters when trying to be more influential the person you most need to start with is yourself. Learn to believe in yourself and come across as confident in what it is you are talking about. The least confident person in the room is almost always going to be the one that ends up with least influence. Start off by talking with confidence. Cut out the umm and err moments. Speak clearly and directly.

Of course no matter how well you communicate if you don't know what you are talking about then this will soon become obvious. Often, even the most confident people fall into the trap of pretending to know something when in fact the opposite is true. If you don't know what you are talking about then shut up. The old adage "better to appear stupid and say nothing than to speak and confirm my stupidity" applies here.

Learn to listen well. We have discussed this earlier but developing good listening skills are important to both gaining influence and persuading others. Training yourself to be interested in others is a useful skill in almost any environment. People love to talk about themselves and their projects. In listening you gain insight as to who they are, what is important to them and at the same time quickly lead them to believe you are interesting simply because you listen. Listening also has the added advantage of showing up another person's weaknesses. You may not want to take advantage of this but at the same time it is better that you know what they are in case you need to work with that person at a later date.

Training yourself to expect the best of people is another fine quality of influence. Sure you are going to be let down from time to time but by expecting the best you subconsciously create in that person the desire to give of their best. Though they may not always deliver you have now placed yourself in a position where you are influencing the behavior of others.

Once you have become known as a good listener with high expectations of others you will find that they begin to seek you out both to solicit your opinion and to use as a sounding board. Don't be scared to dish out praise where it is appropriate but make sure it is genuine. By now your influence will be such that that is what these people will be seeking from you. Your influence levels are increasing. Because you want to remain genuine it is important that you tell the truth now but at the same time steer away from criticism. That does not just mean accepting what they say. It does mean that you need to respond in a positive manner that they will be open to. For example, if a colleague comes to you complaining of a problem with another colleague don't block their complaint or just agree. Instead try offering some suggestion as to how they could deal with that colleague that might be helpful to them.

As your circle of influence develops you will gradually begin to find yourself being places in a position of even greater influence. This can provide dangers in itself but you can deal with it if you remain true to your core principals. For example, you may find yourself being promoted above your work colleagues and this can often lead to resentment and back biting particularly if there is an element of jealousy. Learn to ask questions that will lead someone where you want to go rather than to give orders. Rather than saying to someone to do this, try asking someone if they could do this. If they do, then be sure to give them recognition and lay down the appropriate amount of praise. Use their name in conversations with them. This personalizes the conversation and validates their identity.

Wherever possible, lead with questions that will solicit a yes answer. You may already know the answer to the question but you are giving that person the opportunity to demonstrate that they do and once someone had given a few positive answers it is easier to lead them toward a positive destination that hopefully you had pre-decided upon. One to one meetings generally lead to more open communication and also remove the need for the person you are communicating with to play a role designed more to impress an audience than yourself.

Finally, as your influence grows and you find yourself being placed in positions of increasing authority it is inevitable that you too will make mistakes. Get behind these as quickly as possible and own up to them. People can be more forgiving than you think but if you exacerbate the error by trying to hide it or worse still blame someone else you will increase your problems and reduce your area of influence very quickly. If you are leading any group or team and one of them makes a mistake then by sharing responsibility, even if none of it was yours, then you stand to make huge dividends in terms of loyalty from your team members.

To be effective at influencing others, you must have two things – style and substance. If your foundation of credibility is not solid you will fall and you will fall hard. On the other side of the coin, even those who are very credible can fail if they are not aware of the dynamics at play in the situation.

Studies carried out over 2009 and 2010 identified five categories of styles of influence:

1.　**Asserting -** You have to be insistent that your ideas are heard and you will challenge the ideas that others will have

2.　**Convincing –** You will put your ideas forward in a convincing way. You will offer up sound logical reasoning, rational reasons why others should follow your point of view

3.　**Negotiating –** You will also look for the compromise in a situation and you will concede certain points if it results in the outcome that you want, a satisfying outcome that benefits you

4.　**Bridging –** You will build up relationships and you will connect with other people by listening to them, by understanding what they want, and by building up coalitions where necessary

5.　**Inspiring -** You will strongly advocate the position you come from and you will encourage other people through sharing a sense of purpose and through exciting possibilities.

Each one of these styles can be effective, provided you use it on the right situation and with the right people. One of the most commonly made mistakes is to attempt to use a "one size fits all" approach simply because influencing others is very dependent on situation.

Take a look at these 5 steps to increasing the way you can influence others:

1.   Understand Your Own Style of Influencing

It starts with self-awareness, with understanding what your dominant style is. Are you assertive? Are you convincing? Or do you tend towards negotiation, bridging or inspiring others? Do you use the same approach with every different situation and with every individual? Understanding your own natural style is the best place to begin. Once you understand that, you can move on.

2.   Taking Stock of Your Situation

Ask yourself who the most critical people are that you have to win over in order to achieve your desirable outcome. Then as yourself which style of influence is most likely to have a positive effect. For example, let's say that you are talking to a CEO who is pretty hardnosed and set in his ways. You might consider using the convincing approach, basing your ideas soundly in logic, in expertise and data. Let say, as another example, you are caught in a crisis situation; a situation where you need to be able to thin fast and be decisive; in this case, the assertive influencing style might be more appropriate and effective. If you are working across functions and are looking to gain the support of one or more of your peers, you could use the bridging or the negotiating style of influence.

3. Identify Any Gaps

As soon as you have figured out where your orientation lies and what the right style of influencing s for the situation, it's time to figure out if you can stick to that or if you might need to shift a little and change styles to be more effective.

4. Develop the gap

When you have figured out if there are any gaps that need to be developed, develop them. Go and see a style coach, a role model that you admire or go to a workshop to beef up your knowledge and your own style. Try to find a partner to learn with, someone you can use to role play with to gain more confidence.

5. Practice, Practice and Practice Some More

Start small. Start in low situations where you can put your influencing skills to the test. Target a situation or a person that you would like to see a specific outcome with and have a go. See what is working and what isn't and see where you need to change the style that you are using. As you build up your confidence and get better, move on to bigger situations.

It doesn't matter if you are a leader, a follower, or a collaborator. There is a good chance that you will need to influence a certain number of and type of people if you are to gain success Your strategies can range from a strong reliance on your position to collaboration, encouragement and education. The real key to the door is in knowing which approach you should use in any given situation.

Chapter 4
Mind Control

At first the very term mind control might sound like some sinister plot cooked up by some crackpot totalitarian regime. In fact, we practice mind control every day and it is also practiced on us by just about every marketing company you come across. You are not trying to turn anyone into a mindless zombie, all you want is to persuade someone that your point of view will be to both their benefit and your own. What you are seeking is to persuade someone to be in agreement with yourself.

One of the first principals here is to understand that you must allow them to think. This is not because you are afraid that their thoughts will be contrary to your own but because most people will avoid thinking at all costs. Their plates are already full to overload with all of the day today decisions that life thrusts upon them. The mere fact that you are asking them to consider something new will cause them to batten down the hatches and not make a decision at all. In order to be persuasive you need to do as much of the thinking for them as possible.

Instead of asking a person what they think about something do the thinking for them by lining up all the benefits that will come their way if they pursue the path you are suggesting. Of course you may choose to mention all of the negative possibilities that exist but the fact that you really believe in the path you are suggesting you will be at your most persuasive. Let's return to that beautiful girl standing at the bar sipping chardonnay again. Every guy in the place has his eye on her and you have to convince her to go out with you instead. When you talk to her, naturally you will have timed this with precision, you present her with all the positive reasons there are to accept your invitation. You will treat her as a lady, take her somewhere she would enjoy to go and you promise to make her laugh a lot. That is subtle mind control. You may have forgotten to mention that you don't have a job at the moment and that you are going to need to borrow from your best friend just to take her out but that is a minor detail. You know this has potential to be a win win situation.

Persuading someone to grant you something small can open the door to bigger things. Start with a relatively minor request and once you have got over that hurdle ask for more in ever increasing increments. A person comes into your car show room looking at cars. You don't start the ball rolling by immediately getting him to sign a purchase agreement. Show him a few cars and then suggest he sit in one to try it out for comfort. After that you suggest a test drive and move forward from there. It was that little small step that started the whole ball rolling.

Create some sort of a time scale to increase the need to make a decision. Left to their own devices people will procrastinate rather than make a decision. By creating a deadline, you put them in a position where they have to focus on that decision and not just leave it on the backburner. The problem with this technique is that it is often used by salesmen when they wish to force a sale but the deadline is not real. Create your own deadline but stick to it. If they have not made the decision by the time he deadline expires then remove that option from the table. This may not work in your favor the first time you wish to persuade that person but it sure will the second time and every time after that.

Always remember to give. In fact, you need to be giving constantly, be it in the form of compliments or assistance or just plain old support. In that persons mind you are creating a debt which they not only need to repay, they are so grateful that they want to repay it. When you need them to think you way they are eager to do so.

One of the greatest differences between persuasive people and others is that they are utterly shameless in going after what they want. When they see an opportunity they go for it and if that means asking for something outright then they do it. Where others might hesitate or feel embarrassed the persuasive person does not. This is not because he is more ruthless and self centered. The fact is he believes so whole heartedly in what he is aiming for that he genuinely sees himself as going after the best thing not only for himself but for others as well. If it troubles you to go unashamedly after what you want, then perhaps you need to be asking yourself if it is really something you believe in. Undoubtedly a person is at their most persuasive and is more likely to control the thoughts of others when he is promoting a subject about which he fees passionate. Most of the most powerful and persuasive speeches in our history have been made by people talking about something they believe to be bigger than themselves.

As always timing is important and a person who is tired is much more vulnerable to having his thought processes deviate from what they normally be if he is tired. They may play to our advantage but we need also to be aware that it could also work against us. Just as we may wish to act persuasively there are those who persuade us toward their own agendas and we need to be wary of being put in a position where we have to take decisions when we are not fully at our most alert. Many military type interrogations use sleep deprivation as a tool for exactly this reason.

Other areas where people may try to exhibit mind control over our decision are in advertising. Advertisers are adept are creating a want and then going on to transform that want into something that we perceive as a need. When we see adverts proclaiming that we need something then we need to be aware that this is probably a thinly disguised method of mind control. In general people do not go to advertising agencies when they wish to promote a genuine need. Those tend to be self evident. Instead they promote a want and the it is developed to a point that it has the appearance of a need.

Chapter 5

How to Influence Human Behavior

There are more methods of influencing another human being than one might be aware of. One proven method is that of mirroring or copying the behavior of another person. This takes the form of a type of body language in reverse. Instead of using your body to convey a message you use their body language and play it back to them. By using the same motions, head positions and similar facial expressions it has been proven that you can create a more harmonious relationship with another person. Obviously this makes that person more vulnerable to your being able to influence them and this may be advantageous if you need to persuade that person to take a particular course of action. The problem with mirroring, as it is referred to, is that if the other person detects you doing it then it has the opposite effect to that which was intended and you can lose influence altogether. If you feel this is a tactic that may be useful to you, and I don't want to persuade you here, then you must be at your most discreet. The perception that they are being copied will lead person to conclude that you are mocking him.

Another method that uses a somewhat similar strategy is that of social proof. In other words, if everyone else is doing something then you should too. The fashion industry has traded on this since it began. It is not for no reason that we find that fashion follows trends from year to year. Few people like, or can tolerate, being the odd one out. If straight hair and tight jeans are in this year then nearly everyone will be wearing their hair straight with tight jeans. Of course all you need now do to really reiterate your marketing position is get a well known celebrity to wear tight jeans and straighten their hair and you are away. This phobia of breaking the chain of peer acceptance is very powerful. That is why many advertisements use expressions like "nine out of ten customers found that such and such a product worked wonders for their health" Immediately they have established that this is the thing that most people are doing and the fear of being seen as out of place will kick in automatically. Creating a crowd mentality of one kind or another is an almost guaranteed method of persuading people in a particular direction. It is a method that has been used by politicians, dictators and religious promulgators, almost since those professions came into existence. Once you grasp how this very basic human characteristic works and how wide spread it is then you are able to capitalize on it. If you wish to persuade a child to do something, then first of all you should convince that child that all his friends are doing the same thing. This simple technique relates to the workplace as much as it does to the playground.

Probably some of the most adept people at persuasion are politicians and they love to use this strategy to persuade others. Unfortunately, they are weak when it comes at recognizing when this method is being used against them and that is why you will so often see politicians changing their point of view if they feel that there is a majority going the other way. We need to be aware of this and make sure that our own paths are not influenced by group pressure. As stated earlier in this book our integrity is an important factor in maintaining influence and this may evaporate if we are perceived to sway too much in the direction of the crowd.

Tests have also proven that our influence on others is increased dramatically if we are perceived to be an authority in a certain area. Having recognized qualifications displayed on the wall of an office has been shown to increase the authority that a person is perceived to have. It goes much further though. If somebody describes you as an authority in a certain subject, then your status will be elevated and your persuasiveness increases. It has even been shown that even if the third party promoting your expertise is somebody you know well, the mere fact that they speak highly of you will influence the other person's perception of you. Advertising agencies like to use a doctor or dentist to promote medical or dental products as many people will believe that their endorsement proves the product is effective. Often these medical professionals are nothing other than actors with white coats on. Hopefully you won't need to stoop to that level but if you can persuade someone to put in a good word for you it may not be a bad idea. As people come to accept you as an authority in one area they will be more ready to accept you as an authority in other areas. I once had a job teaching English in the Himalayas. Teachers are highly respected there and soon people were coming to me with broken pumps and motorcycles because they assumed that I must also have been an expert in other areas. (Sadly they were mistaken)

Influencing others is also a matter of being able to pick out other key influencers in a group and harness their power. If you are working with a group of people it is a waste of time to try persuading one of the less influential members of something if they are only going to be swayed by someone else coming along with a contrary line of thought. Instead you need to focus your efforts on the most influential people in the knowledge that if you can win them over to your idea then the battle is half won.

Chapter 6
Mind Reading

Mind reading is a very controversial subject brought into disrepute by the many charlatans, suspense films and television dramas that depict this as some sort of dark mysterious art. For the purposes of this publication it may be better to think in terms of emotional or mood interpretation. In fact, science is only now beginning to get to grips with our ability if not to mind read, then at least to be able to interpret the feelings and emotions of others. It has recently been discovered that we have an area within our brains that actively tries to replicate the emotion of people we are interacting with.

In basic terms we are observing others and attempting to walk in their emotional shoes in a figurative way. This is nothing new and most of us practice it to a certain extent in our day to day lives. Children are able to interpret when their parents are angry whilst a husband may know his wife is feeling unwell even if she has not voiced any complaint. This emotional recognition is normally generated because we are dealing with someone with whom we are very familiar but the skills can be developed to work with anyone if we are open to trying and willing to put in the time to do so. It is an unfortunate indictment of our fast paced lives that we have lost much of this talent simply because we are so often in such a hurry that we don't use this ability anymore.

A good place to start is a person's facial expression. We often wear our mood on our faces and if you make an effort to observe someone carefully then you will gain a good deal of information about the way they are feeling. Of course the moment we detect we are being observed we try to disguise our emotions and so it is necessary to hide the fact that you are watching someone. Never study their face for more than a few seconds at a time but do so deliberately and with the intention of assessing their mood. As you practice this you will find you become better at it. At the same time notice their body language but only to confirm what you are reading in their face. You are not attempting to become an expert in the art of body language here but it will soon be obvious if they are slumped down and depressed looking or rigid with anger. This amalgamation of physical displays, though quite unintentional on the part of the person displaying them, will help you develop a better understanding of that person at any given time.

Once you have taken the time to get to know a person and have started to have a better understanding of how they function in both an emotional and physical way more insights will become obvious. If a person becomes withdrawn perhaps there is some sort of problem. If a person is being more gregarious and loud perhaps he is trying to impress someone or angling for promotion.

It is hard to overstate the benefits of just watching the people with whom you interact. In every way you should be developing your ability to quietly detach yourself from your environment and observe. This will teach you all sorts of things about a person and the group dynamics that surround you. All of this is vital information that you will be able to use to your own benefit when the time is right for you to make persuasive moves.

Some of the information you glean from you study of people will just be filed away for use at a later stage. Other information should be acted upon perhaps to build relationships. If you detect, for example, that one of your work colleagues is depressed then at an appropriate time perhaps you should gently ask a few questions. Remember to remain sensitive and empathetic but by putting yourself in a position to give emotional support you are building a bridge. If things go well you will have someone at your back when it comes time to use your persuasive powers and this is important from a number of angles.

1 When you put forward a suggestion you already have someone that is likely to support you.

2 You have started, therefore, to develop a group dynamic that others will lean toward.

3 Hopefully as a result of your intervention he perceives you as trustworthy.

4 The person is likely to say positive things about you that will increase your credibility.

5 That person has a feeling of indebtedness toward you that he is anxious to repay.

All in all, the act of studying people with whom you are dealing and by reading their emotional state you will develop a better understanding of their behavioral patterns that will prove useful to you at some later stage. Providing you act on that gleaned information with the correct attitude and at the appropriate time the benefits can be enormous and all at the cost of just stepping back and observing for a few minutes. The more you understand them, the better your chances of persuading them to follow your leadership at some time in the future.

Chapter 7

The Persuasive Power of Fear

Fear is an extremely powerful tool that has been used and abused by ruthless people for years. Fear is not a pleasant emotion but is one of the most powerful of all emotions using the threat of danger, pain or harm.

The Nazis are probably the greatest example of persuasion by fear in recent history. "The best political weapon, is the weapon of terror. Cruelty commands respect. Men may hate us. But, we don't ask for their love; only for their fear." Heinrich Himmler.

Many leaders and tyrants have understood the power of fear and have used it as a method to control others for their own benefit. Fear is contagious and used ruthlessly has immense power to persuade people to proceed along paths they may not normally have taken. Although this dynamic is most obvious when used by military and political tyrants it can often be seen to a lesser extent being used in corporate, religious, family or marital environments.

The sheer power of the fear mechanism, when used by those ruthless enough to do so, can be enormous. It should not only be seen in a negative light as it can be incredibly productive when harnessed correctly. An example may be the results that a team of workers can come up with when under the fear of not meeting a dead line for example.

The person who uses this method of persuasion needs to be extremely cautious however. Fear produces a fight or flight reaction and is not often conducive to true loyalty. Sure you may be able to encourage a team to rush off and produce incredible results when under pressure. Understand, though, they are going to resent having been placed under this pressure and when the time comes that they feel they should fight then you had better be watching your own back because there is not likely to be anyone there to watch it for you.

As a tool fear has its place but those who choose it as the main weapon in their armory, often find that they lead from a lonely position as the only loyalty comes from those whom they are most able to intimidate. People may follow out of fear but they will resent the person who causes that fear. The result is usually short term gain which disintegrates when the fear dissipates. This means that constant stress has to be applied to the people being intimidated or the whole relationship will fall apart.

Conversely building loyalty may not show the same short term benefits as it requires much more effort, time and vulnerability on the part of those attempting to build it. It also needs a higher level of trust between both parties or groups but when properly developed creates a far stronger and more enduring bond. It also allows for greater input from all parties which can produce a wider more all encompassing result. This contrast between developing fear or developing loyalty is something you will need to weigh up in your own relationships and the persuasive tactics you choose to pursue.

Chapter 8
10 Ways to Positively Influence Others in Your Workplace

It doesn't matter how hard you work or how brilliant you are, you cannot succeed in anything with help and without cooperation from other people. We are not individuals; we are all connected to one another in some way. The world is actually shrinking as, at the touch of a button, the click of a mouse, we can keep up with and keep in contact with even the most remote parts of our globe and we can learn from other cultures as easily as we learn from our own. No matter which part of the world we come from, we are not so different. We all have the same needs, as does any stranger that we meet. The same thin can also be said about the people that we work with.

It doesn't matter where you work and it doesn't matter what you do for a living, we all have one thing in common – a large part of our waking hours are spent in our workplaces, some of us in jobs that we like and some in jobs that we hate.

If you are the latter, if you are working at a place, doing a job that you simply don't like, you can make your life much more bearable by persuading people to be on your side; you might even find that you quite enjoy going to work after all.

Here are 10 ways that you can positively influence other people in your workplace and make life so much easier to bear:

1.   Be Grateful

Or at least get into the habit of being grateful. Before you leave home every morning, look round at what you have and say the words "thank you". Be thankful that you have a home, maybe a car, food on the table and a family to share it with. One you learn to appreciate what you have, your purpose will become much clearer – to bring home the money to pay for it all, the money that the job you hate pays you every week or month. As the day goes on and you face challenges that seem insurmountable, reflect on your gratefulness. It will make you happier and it will make it easier for you to carry on.

2.   Be Happy

Happiness truly is contagious and there are, in all truthfulness, more than a billion reason to be happy. We weren't put on the earth to be miserable so find a reason to be happy. Rejoice in the sky, the sun, the rain that gives life. Talk to your colleagues, the people who help you through each day at work; smile at those who don't help you. If you are alive and you are healthy then you are doing okay. If you are happy others will be happy too.

3.   Keep on Smiling

Even if you don't feel like it. There is an old expression, "fake it until you make it" and it has never been truer, especially when things go wrong. No matter what is happening, no matter how bad you feel, smile and you will feel better. If the boss is on your back, you co-workers are not pulling their weight, your computer crashed and wiped out everything you did, just smile. There is actually a scientific reason for it – smiling helps to release endorphins in the blood and these are not called happy hormones for nothing. Smiling also eases tension, not just in you but in those around you as well. People will notice, they will begin smiling and the tension will ease. You and you alone will have persuaded everyone that everything is ok, with just a smile.

4.   Always Say Your Pleases and Thank Yous

Good manners get you a long way and help to build up better relationships. This isn't just about the workplace, this works anywhere you go, to a restaurant, the movies, the grocery store. Be polite and show manners and people will do what they can to help you. In the workplace, your colleagues will more be likely to help you out if you are polite and treat them with the respect and courtesy you expect from them. Good manners show that you care so make it a habit to treat others as you want to be treated.

5.   Steer Clear of the Gossip

At any given moment of the day, something will be happening in your workplace that give people a reason to talk, to gossip about someone else behind their back. It is human nature to talk about things that happen but the nature of gossip s that is often becomes distorted, purely for entertainment value, and all else is lot. Gossip is demoralizing to the subject and it can also be classed as bullying if it turns malicious. If you happen to be in a place where people are gossiping and they try to draw you in, just smile at them and then walk away. Show them you will not become involved and avoid the negativity. Not only does it keep you stabilized, it will also stop you form, wrongly, judging the victim and will also gain you respect from others.

6.   Be Nice to the "Village Idiot"

It doesn't matter where you work, there will always be the "village idiot". This is perhaps a very cruel term because the victim of that term is, more often than not, merely eccentric, different from others, not so articulate. It doesn't make them an actual idiot. Whenever you have cause to speak to them, be nice to them, listen to what they have to say and you might just be surprised at how un-idiot like they actually are. Too often, we label people unfairly and, by taking the tie to include them, to listen to them, you are developing a large amount of good will. You don't know when you may need to call on people for help so make sure you keep them on your side.

7. Be Diplomatic

Everywhere you go, there will be people who say or do things that cause irritation. The real key is to stay objective and to stay calm. Losing your temper, or choosing to be angry as your very first reaction will do nothing more than provide the fire with a much needed fuel source to keep on irritating you. Allow it to happen, and your colleagues will lose all respect for you. It doesn't matter how hard it is not to respond, when people say things that are hurtful or simply irritating, do not respond. Remain in control, remain calm and you will be left alone. If you can muster one, smile at them and then continue with what you were doing. And if you do have to say something, keep your voice soft, and lam, be kind to them. It is your anger that they want and if you don't give it, they have nothing, You, on the other hand, will gain the respect of your colleagues.

8. Do Your Very Best All of the Time

Your bosses and any colleagues who are influential will respect you more if you always do the very best that you can. Even if you are at odds with people, doing your best, putting in your effort, will result in milestones being reached and deadline met. People may not like you for one reason or another but they can still respect you for being someone they can depend on, someone who remains focused. You will also have a better sense of self-worth and purpose. It may result in a raise or promotion or it could just mean that you are in a better position to influence others in the future.

9.   Always Be Honest

Honesty is always the very best policy and, when you add diplomacy into the mx, you have the makings of a great communicator, a true leader. When you are trying to talk to others about your ideas, keep to the facts; don't throw in a lot of technical jargon and don't try to be too smart – it will backfire on you. Never exaggerate your claim, and never embellish them as people can see through that and your chances of persuading them round to your way of thinking will be gone. It isn't always the contents of the message that work; it is the way the message is conveyed.

10.   Respect Other Cultures

The world is multicultural and, no matter where you live and work, you will come across people of different ethnicities and different cultures. Get to know them, get to know their traditions, beliefs, food choices and develop a respect for them. Each different ultra has something that we can all learn from and it is our duty, our moral duty to show them respect. Walk away from racist conversations; f you stay, if you join in, you are no better than they are. Having that kind of name does not help you to be able to influence others and everyone will lose a little of their respect for you. No matter where you go, no matter which nationalities you come across there will be good people and bad. Focus your energies on the good in all of us and you will find that people are more prepared to cooperate with you, to follow where you want to lead them.

These may not seem like ways to persuade people but think about everything I have said carefully. By being nice to others, showing respect and remaining calm and dependable, you are turning yourself into someone that others will trust in, that they will want to follow.

Chapter 9

How to Persuade People

Do you want to know how you can persuade people so that you can get whatever you want?

Usually, the one thing that separates a successful person from everyone else is the power of influence. The following are some of the tactics that have great potential in helping you to increase your persuasive powers. These tactics are not plucked out of thin air; they have been proven through psychological research.

How to persuade a skeptic - be confident and talk fast

The very best way to persuade your audience, especially if they are definitely not agreeing with you, s to speed up your pace of talking. Listen to someone who is talking fast; don't you find it distracting? Can you actually hear or pic out any flaws in the argument? Thought not. The opposite is also true; when you are talking with an audience that is definitely on your side, slow down your speech, let them hear exactly what you are saying and give them the time they need to agree with you a little bit more.

Talking with confidence is also a great way to boost your persuasive power. In fact, it has been proven, beyond a doubt that confidence is even better than accuracy when it comes to earning trust from other people. Most people prefer to take advice and learn from someone who is confident, even going so far as to forgive and forget about a poor track record in someone who exudes confidence. Unfortunately, in a competitive situation, this can result in some people who offer advice, who want people to follow them, exaggerating just how confident they really are.

It is a natural thing to associate confidence and expertise. If you truly know your product or service, if you are confident of the facts about the benefits and you truly believe that it does what it says, you will be naturally confident. In order to successfully persuade others, you need to be able to communicate your confidence, well, confidently.

- **Swearing can actually persuade your audience**

Just light swearing of course. If you go overboard and litter your words with profanity, you will lose all of your credibility and any respect your audience may have had for you. Recently, researchers gathered 88 participants and split them into three groups. Each group was to watch one of three speeches, each slightly different. The only real difference was that one of the speech included a mild swear word at the beginning of it. The second speech had the mild swear word at the end of it and the third had none at all.

When the researchers measured the attitudes of each group of participants, they found that they were influenced the most by the speeches that included the curse word, in this case, the words used were "damn it". Use of the word "damn" resulted in the audience taking more notice of the intensity of the speech and that resulted in an increase in persuasion. None of the three groups changed the way they perceived the speaker's credibility, just the speech they were giving, proving that a little mild swearing can do wonders for your power of persuasion.

• Get them to agree with you about something

If you really want to persuade someone to do what you want them to do, begin by giving them something that they can actually agree with. In a stud carried out by Robert Wyre and Jing Xu, they discovered that there are certain effects of any message that people tend to agree with. In one test, the students listened to a speech given by John McCain r by Barack Obama and then go on to watch a Toyota TV ad.

The republicans in the group were more easily swayed by the advert after they watched John McCain, while the democrats were persuaded after watching President Obama.

When you attempt to sell something, be it a service, a product, or an idea, come up with a statement or a view that your audience can definitely agree with and get it out there in the open right at the start, even if it has nothing to do with the idea you are selling.

- **A balanced argument is more persuasive**

If what you are saying or selling is likely to inspire criticism, do not, under any circumstances, cover up the weakness or flaws in your arguments. We all fear that, by talking about a flaw or a weakness we are undermining our own point of view but, in actual fact, it is the opposite. The following is taken from Psyblog:

Over the years psychologists have compared one-sided and two-sided arguments to see which are the most persuasive in different contexts. Daniel O'Keefe at the University of Illinois collected together the results of 107 different studies on sidedness and persuasion conducted over 50 years which, between them, recruited 20,111 participants (O'Keefe, 1999, Communication Yearbook, 22, pp. 209-249).

The results of this meta-analysis provide persuasive reading. What he found across different types of persuasive messages and with varied audiences, was that two-sided arguments are more persuasive than their one-sided equivalents.

On the whole, people aren't stupid. Knowing how to persuade them means that you are acknowledging that they know how to think. If you omit to mention the other side of the argument, your audience will now that and they are less likely to believe in what you are saying. If necessary, mention the downsides or the shortfalls in your product or service on your website.

• **Seeing is believing**

People will definitely believe you more if they can see the evidence with their own eyes. Research carried out by Eric Johnson, Ye Li and Lisa Zaval looked at global warning and how it was related to the local weather at the time.

Participants in studies in both Australia and the US were asked to rate how strong they believed in global warming. They were also asked to rate if the temperature that day was colder, warmer or normal for the time of the year. When they felt that it was warmer, they believed more in global warming than when they said it was colder than normal.

In another, related, study, the same questions were asked but, at the same time, the participants were also asked to make a donation to a non-profit organization that was working to combat global warming. When the day was perceived to be warmer, participants in the study donated more than 4 times the amount of money that they did when the day was perceived to be colder than normal.

What comes out of that is this – if you want to persuade people to follow you, to believe in your message, you must ask them to do so in the right situation that supports your claims. Online, you should use storytelling, emotional design an imagery to build up the stage for the story you want to sell.

- **Upsell products that are 60% lower in cost**

Once you have a customer that is at the point where they are going to buy from you, they have put their trust in you and have persuaded themselves that it is okay to buy from you, to give you their money. At that point you will find it much easier to sell them more.

Let's say that someone purchases a shirt from you. Upsell with an tem that costs 60% of the original price, i.e. add a tie in, not the entire suit. There is a time tested rule which dictates customers will buy any upsell for 60% of the time, for a cost of up to 60% of their original purchase price. If you are not using upselling, do so now, you might be surprised at how easy it is to persuade people to buy more.

- **Frame the Positive**

When you emphasize the positives in your message, you will find that they are far more positive than pointing out any negative. The results from 29 different studies wee analyzed. These studies were carried out on a total number of 6738 people and the findings were that there was a slightly more persuasive advantage in giving a positively framed message than there was in a negative one.

These studies were to do with way the participants related to the prevention of disease. The ideas promoted included encouraging people to use more sunscreen, and eating a healthier diet but the ideas behind it could be used for a much wider appeal. The researchers came up with the thought that the reasoning behind it is that people do not like to feel they are being bullied into changing the way they live or behave so framing the message in a positive way would have more effect than banging on about the negatives.

Try it for yourself, frame your message in a more positive way and see how much difference it really makes.

•   **The Strange Paradox of Choice**

Think about it – the more you have to offer, the less likely people are to take you up on things. A study was carried out in a jam tasting stall, set up inside an upmarket Californian supermarket. Occasionally just 6 flavors of jam were offered while at others there were 24. Tasters were then given a voucher to go and buy some jam at a discount price.

More choice of jams attracted far more customers, but most of them only looked; very few actually bought any jam. The stall that offered the limited number of tastings actually made more sales – significantly more. On the 24 jam stall, only 3% of those who tasted actually spent their voucher; on the 6 jam stall, that went up to 30%.

The message here is, if you have a lot of products or a lot of ideas, spend time filtering them so that you only offer a limited range, what people want to be persuaded to buy into.

- **Repetition is Key**

If you see something or hear something enough, you will eventually be persuaded to buy into it. Repetition has a very distinct effect on the human race. Adverts that are repeated over and over will automatically play in your mind when you see the product; songs that are played repeatedly will grow on you eventually. Repetition of words or patterns causes it to not only be remembered but to accept that what you hear or see is actually the truth.

The following comes from Changing Minds and it is concerned with the persuasion research that Hugh Rank did in 1976:

Our brains are excellent pattern-matchers and reward us for using this very helpful skill. Repetition creates a pattern, which consequently and naturally grabs our attention.

Repetition creates familiarity, but does familiarity breed contempt? Although it can happen, the reality is that familiarity leads to liking in far more case than it does to contempt. When we are in a supermarket, we are far more likely to buy familiar brands, even if we have never tried the product before.

Think about the last time you bought a pair of shoes. Did you pick them then put them down several times before trying them on. Did you come back to try them again? If so, you are in good company. Many people have to repeat things several times before they get convinced. Three times is a common number.

Repeat your key benefits or key parts of your message many times over. Effective campaigns do just that but keep it friendly. One more piece of research shows that, out of a whole group, if just one person repeats their opinion often enough, it will eventually be seen as the representative opinion of the entire group.

- **Men respond better to emails than face to face**

Research carried out in 2002 showed that men appear to be far more responsive to email than they do with face to face talk. This is because it bypasses their tendencies to be competitive. Conversely women respond better to face to face talk because they tend to be ore "relationship-minded".

The research suggests that, while email could be a way of reaching more men, by getting past the competition side of their nature, it will only apply if the relationship is distant. If a man has a close relationship, face to face works better. If you want to persuade a man to do something and you don't know him very well, try email first.

- **Limited purchasing power makes you buy more**

This really is true. If you are selling, let's say, athletic socks, and people can buy as many pairs as they want, you will find that the average order is quite low. If, however, you limit the number of pairs that each person can buy you will find that they actually buy the maximum amount. This is because they now they are getting a bargain and are subconsciously scared that they may not be able to get any more.

Brian Wansink wrote a book called "Mindless Eating: Why We Eat More Than We Think" and he had this to say:

A while back, I teamed up with two professor friends of mine— Steve Hoch and Bob Kent—to see if anchoring influences how much food we buy in grocery stores. We believed that grocery shoppers who saw numerical signs such as "Limit 12 Per Person" would buy much more than those who saw signs such as "No Limit Per Person."

To nail down the psychology behind this, we repeated this study in different forms, using different numbers, different promotions (like "2 for $2" versus "1 for $1"), and in different

supermarkets and convenience stores. By the time we finished,
we knew that almost any sign with a number promotion leads
us to buy 30 to 100 percent more than we normally would.

Limiting the amount that people can buy will definitely make them buy more.

- ### Stories Beat Data Hands Down

Back in 2007, Carnegie Mellon University carried out a study on the effect of story against data. The researchers were George Lowenstein Deborah Small and Paul Slovic. The subjects were asked to go around collecting donation for a really bad situation that was happening in Africa. The data pitch that they were given was full of statistics about bad shortages of food in Malawi, about the severe lack of rainfall in Zambia and how millions of people has been dislocated in Angola.

The second version of the pith talked of a specific person, a little, starving girl in Zambia, called Rokia. Her phot was shown and people were asked to donate towards her direct help.

On average, those who saw the first pitch, the data-based pitch, donated $1.14 while those who were shown the story-based pitch donated an average of $2.38, more than double the amount.

A third test was carried out; students were told of Rokia, of her plight but they were also told of the statistics about the drought, the shortages of food and the starving millions. Compared to the average of $2.38 that the second group donated, those who read of Rokia's plight and the statistics donated an average amount of $1.43.

The message here is that too much data is overwhelming; because it is such a large problem, most people feel that what they donate cannot make a difference and only donate a small amount. Mother Theresa once said, "if I look at the mass I will never act. If I look at the one, I will".

- *If you are selling to men, use photos of women*

This one really does make sense if you think about it and a field study, carried out in the consumer credit market, showed that sing images of women was as effective as dropping the interest rate right down. A lender from South Africa sent out letters, offering short term loans at a randomly generated rate of interest. Those letters also contained a number of psychological features, also randomized. As was expected, the interest rate had a significant impact on whether the loan was taken up or not. What was surprising was that, at complete odds with standard economics, some of the random psychological features also had an effect.

The lending company had this to say about their study:

For the male customers, replacing the photo of a male with a photo of female on the offer letter statistically significantly increases take up; the effect is about as much as dropping the interest rate 4.5 percentage points... For female customers, we find no statistically significant patterns.

Overall, these results suggest a very powerful effect on male customers of seeing a female photo on the offer letter. Standard errors however do not allow us to isolate one specific mechanism for this effect. The effect on male customers may be due to either the positive impact of a female photo or the negative impact of a male photo.

The letters that were sent out were rather drastic in their range of interest rate, with people receiving offers of anywhere between 3.25% and 11.75%. For those that had a photo of a woman on the letter, the effect was the equivalent of a 4.5% difference in the interest rate.

Next time you are targeting an audience of men, use a picture or image of a woman ad you will see a significant rise in conversions. It doesn't have to be a bikini-clad woman with an hourglass figure either, although that may help

Why does this work? Research shows that, when they become aroused, men become stupid because it makes them very bad at making decisions. They seem to get tunnel vision but, interestingly enough, this tunnel vision only lasts for as long as it takes to make the purchase. Once the deed is done and the image of the woman is no longer in sight, nor considered to be important, the effect will disappear, making it nothing more than a short-term one.

Studies also show that using a sexy advert for your product will not make men any more likely to remember the advert. At the end of the day, they are so focused on the sexy woman on the ad, they don't know or care what the product is or the brand it carries. If you want them to remember the actual brand you are trying to persuade them to buy into you will need to come up with something a bit more substantial.

Chapter 10
Persuasive Quotes

To end, the following are some of the more persuasive of all the quotes on the subject of persuasion and all, in one way or another, reinforce what has been taught in this book.

"If you wish to win a man over to your ideas, first make him your friend." **Abraham Lincoln**

"That which we do not believe, we cannot adequately say; even though we may repeat the words ever so often." **Ralph Waldo Emerson**

"The most important persuasion tool you have in your entire arsenal is integrity". Zig **Ziegler**

"You may fool all the people some of the time, you can even fool some of the people all of the time, but you cannot fool all of the people all the time." **Abraham Lincoln**

"People are usually more convinced by reasons they discovered themselves than by those found out by others." **Blaise Pascal**

"I don't know the rules of grammar. If you're trying to persuade people to do something, or buy something, it seems to me you should use their language." **David Ogilvy**

"When a person is determined to believe something, the very absurdity of the doctrine confirms them in their faith." **Junius**

"Persuasion is better than force." **Anon**

"You might as well fall flat on your face as lean over too far backward". **James Thurber**

"If you can't get people to listen to you any other way, tell them it's confidential." **Anon**

"The tongue can paint what the eye can't see." - **Anon**

"That which proves too much, proves nothing!" **Anon**

"The persuasion of a friend is a strong thing" **Homer**

"Call the bald man, Boy; make the sage thy toy; greet the youth with solemn face; praise the fat man for his grace." **Helen Rowland**

"There is a holy, mistaken zeal in politics, as well as in religion. By persuading others, we convince ourselves." **Junius**

"The object of oratory alone in not truth, but persuasion." **Thomas Babington Macaulay, 1st Baron Macaulay**

"As there is no worse lie than a truth misunderstood by those who hear it, so reasonable arguments, challenges to magnanimity, and appeals to sympathy or justice, are folly when we are dealing with human crocodiles and boa-constrictors." **William James**

"Why harass with eternal purposes a mind too weak to grasp them?" **Horace**

"Whenever he met a great man he groveled before him, and my-lorded him as only a free-born Briton can do." **William Makepeace Thackeray**

"When a heart is on fire, sparks always fly out of the mouth." **Anon**

"He that winna be ruled by the rudder man be ruled by the rock." **Anon**

"If you would convince others, seem open to conviction yourself." **Anon**

"To make converts is the natural ambition of everyone." **Johann Wolfgang von Goethe**

"Hence to fight and conquer in all your battles is not supreme excellence; supreme excellence consists in breaking the enemy's resistance without fighting." **Sun Tzu**

"Not brute force but only persuasion and faith are the kings of this world." **Thomas Carlyle**

"Those that will not hear must be made to feel." **Anon**

"More flies are caught with honey than with vinegar." **Anon**

"Who speaks to the instincts speaks to the deepest in mankind, and finds the readiest response." **Amos Bronson Alcott**

"If I have said something to hurt a man once, I shall not get the better of this by saying many things to please him." **Samuel Johnson**

"Let one who wants to move and convince others, first be convinced and moved themselves. If a person speaks with genuine earnestness the thoughts, the emotion and the actual condition of their own heart, others will listen because we all are knit together by the tie of sympathy." **Thomas Carlyle**

"Remember that what pulls the strings is the force hidden within; there lies the power to persuade, there the life -- there, if one must speak out, the real man." **Marcus Aurelius**

"He makes people pleased with him by making them first pleased with themselves." **Anon**

"Nothing is so unbelievable that oratory cannot make it acceptable." **Cicero**

"The art of pleasing consists in being pleased." **William Hazlitt**

"People have a peculiar pleasure in making converts, that is, in causing others to enjoy what they enjoy, thus finding their own likeness represented and reflected back to them." **Johann Wolfgang von Goethe**

"Oral delivery aims at persuasion and making the listener believe they are converted. Few persons are capable of being convinced; the majority allow themselves to be persuaded." **Johann Wolfgang von Goethe**

"The real persuaders are our appetites, our fears and above all our vanity. The skillful propagandist stirs and coaches these internal persuaders." **Eric Hoffer**

"If you would persuade, you must appeal to interest rather than intellect." **Benjamin Franklin**

"Secrecy has many advantages, for when you tell someone the purpose of any object right away, they often think there is nothing to it." **Johann Wolfgang von Goethe**

"Roughly speaking, any man with energy and enthusiasm ought to be able to bring at least a dozen others round to his opinion in the course of a year no matter how absurd that opinion might be. We see every day in politics, in business, in social life, large masses of people brought to embrace the most revolutionary ideas, sometimes within a few days. It is all a question of getting hold of them in the right way and working on their weak points." **Aleister Crowley**

"He who wants to persuade should put his trust not in the right argument, but in the right word. The power of sound has always been greater than the power of sense." **Joseph Conrad**

"I would rather try to persuade a man to go along, because once I have persuaded him, he will stick. If I scare him, he will stay just as long as he is scared, and then he is gone." **Dwight D. Eisenhower**

"To convert somebody go and take them by the hand and guide them." **Thomas Aquinas**

"Would you persuade, speak of interest, not of reason." **Benjamin Franklin**

Conclusion

Whether or not we recognize it, we are exposed to persuasion techniques and we use persuasion on a regular basis. This may take the form of a high powered marketing presentation to the wording of a simple heartfelt love letter. We are bombarded with messages from politicians to leaflets telling us about the latest and greatest pizza deals and no matter how you choose to dress it up, it is all about persuasion. One might argue that the very need for communication grew out of a desire to persuade others.

We have seen that the ability to persuade is one of the most crucial ingredients in our dealings with people if we are to have any sort of influence and do not want to be relegated to the role of camp follower for the rest of our lives. The greater our ability is to persuade others the better we will be at whatever field it is we are pursuing, be it social, business or recreational. At first glance some of the tactics we have looked at may seem manipulative but when examined in greater depth we soon see that really persuasive people are sensitive to the needs and feelings of others and in order to remain in roles where they continue to have the greatest influence they need to be able to generate high levels of loyalty and respect. Doing this requires sensitivity, integrity and excellent communication skills.

It is not sufficient to simply persuade people to follow you once or twice. In order to gain influence, we need to establish ourselves as persuasive on an ongoing basis. This requires trust, credibility and a high degree of empathy for the needs of others. We have seen the result of fear generated persuasive techniques used by dictators and despots the world over. In the long term these tactics always crumble and leave behind deep bitterness and animosity.

The true giants of our society have all been highly persuasive but yet have not had to resort to fear generating or manipulating techniques to persuade the world to the worthiness of their causes. In many ways our commonality is greater and more broad reaching than we realize and it is the ability to communicate that common bond that exists between us that separates the great persuaders from the despots.

As you may know, a great skill that helps you influence people is **Body language**.

This is so important, that I decided to give you a free preview of my book *Body Language Training*.

You'll find it in the next chapter, so go ahead and read it.

Enjoy your gift!

Finally, if you enjoyed this book, then why don't you leave a review on Amazon, just like all the other customers did? Your opinion is important in order to make this guide better and better. I really appreciate your feedback!

Good luck my friend,

Robert Moore

Preview of "Body Language Training"

The 10 Principles of High Status Body Language

Now I will show you different high status body language positions and principles.

First of all, understand that as a high status man, you will always make yourself comfortable first, wherever you go. That's not a selfish behavior, since it will give everyone else around you the permission to relax, feel good and be comfortable too.

#1 principle: take up more space.

Low status people tend to make themselves small, invisible, sitting or standing in an uncomfortable way. They are not sending their energy out to the world, because they don't see themselves as high status people: in their mind they're not worth it.

They're closed on themselves. They're hiding from the outside world. This is apparent by crossing their legs or squeezing them together when they sit. They cross their hands in their lap or arms over their chest, slumping their shoulders or neck forward, or looking down.

You, on the other hand, will think that your energy is so valuable that of course you're willing to share it with the world, so you're going to open yourself and take up more space.

Spread your legs and your arms: be comfortable!

There have been several studies done on the primal nature of our natural body language and what that message conveys to the world. They observations have been unanimous and synonymous around the world, not just in the human kingdom but the animal kingdom as well.

Open, wide body poses and positions are far more reflecting of dominance. They also portray confidence and personal comfort. When you are comfortable with yourself, it shows because you are less reactionary and more responsive; less tense and more relaxed. This has a natural effect to confide and calm others around you. They will feel it from you and tend to adjust themselves accordingly, following your lead.

Closed off body postures such as the ones described previously send messages of insecurity, unworthiness, discomfort, and lack of confidence. This especially goes for people who tend to touch the neck area, which is a severe sign of insecurity or feeling unsafe, whether just by themselves or in their surroundings. These people tend to be less successful simply because they do not think of themselves as successful. It might seem that it's the other way around – they do not think themselves successful because they are less successful overall – but this is not true.

Anyone who puts their full effort into something and sees it through to giving their all, whether they fail or actually succeed in the end is still a success. Investing in yourself to be the best person you possibly can be is the most successful move you can make.

If they fail at first, it's necessary to keep trying and try in different ways. If multiple earnest tries in one way simply do not produce any results, it's necessary to change up the approach and try again from a different angle. Doing the same thing and expecting different results is Einstein's explanation of insanity.

These people who carry themselves in a closed off way have not tried, give up after a few attempts or have not put their full effort into trying. They tend to make excuses for themselves. The real reason they are considered low status is because their thoughts put them there, but this doesn't make it true about them. They always have the potential to change and amaze.

Another interesting principle that has arisen out of university research on the effect of certain body postures is the hormones in the body that are stimulated differently based on the different poses. In order to illustrate the results of these findings, you should first know about cortisol, the "stress hormone", if you don't already.

When we feel mental or physical strain, it can be from any number of different stimuli, although mental stress ultimately always results because of that particular viewpoint that regards something as "stressful". By seeing it another way, the stress is removed.

When we do feel stress, the production of cortisol is triggered. It is closely associated with the emotions of fear and anxiety. It deals with the adrenal glands, designed to assist the body and primitive mind in survival with an extra surge of potent energy. The problem is that this energy is not lasting, and the body must recuperate from the excess secretion of it.

A build-up of cortisol in the body is often due to prolonged or unresolved stress. If left unchecked, it causes detrimental effects. Stress remains in the body, affecting the performance of the muscles, as well as straining and cramping them. Excessive cortisol can keep you anxious and frustrated. If prolonged for long enough time it can begin to damage other important organs and systems of the body, such as seeing the dystrophy of nerves. This can leave a person suffering from excessive amounts of cortisol to develop further, more serious complications. It adds to a constant feeling of pain and discomfort.

Physical exercise has been proven time and time again to reduce cortisol levels. Go out for a 20 minute walk at the very least and notice how different you feel afterward. 20 minutes of cardio significantly reduces cortisol levels. What else reduces cortisol? Power poses!

Standing over a table with your palms flat on the table and arms wide, leaning in forward a bit is a great power pose. Sitting back and opening your arms, folding your hands behind your head is another one. Sitting with wide legs and open arms is another still. Standing with your legs slightly wider than your hips and your hands on your hips with your arms out at your sides is known as "the superman" power pose.

These wide, open and confident poses have actually been proven to stimulate the production of testosterone in both males and females. Testosterone helps to reduce cortisol and increase serotonin production – the "happy hormone". It also adds to a boost of confidence.

Experiments have been done by having people practice these power poses for two minutes before taking mock job interviews that they were unaware of being staged. Another group was asked to hold a closed off, insecure pose for 2 minutes before such an interview.

From the results of the interviews, it was observed that the people who held insecure poses were not any less-qualified candidates for the job, but they were remarked as being less appealing candidates because of their quiet or withdrawn manner.

The people who had held power poses two minutes before the interview were noted as being engaging, confident, a pleasure to talk to, as well as interesting and appealing enough to be asked in for a second interview or be offered a job.

So when it comes to figuring out how you are used to carrying yourself, use the body awareness you've developed and simply ask yourself: "am I closed or open right now?"

You'll know the answer: take action and open up the positioning of your body.

#2 principle: show your crotch.

Dominant men who attract, seduce and fu*k a lot of girls, have no problem showing their sexuality to the world.

So, don't be afraid to draw attention to the crotch region of your body while you're sitting. Open your legs, maybe put a hand in that region to subconsciously draw attention there; showing a nice belt can help you, too.

Aren't your proud of who you are?

Aren't you proud of your body and your incredibly energetic, attractive sex drive?

Always show your pride: be a MAN, be proud of your sexuality.

What's more than that, be a GENTLEMAN and express your raw maleness with a refined candor.

#3 principle: slow down your movements.

Move slower!

Low status people move quickly and fidgety, they're not comfortable, they don't believe in themselves.

From now on, you'll cut your movements in half.

When you're walking, when you're turning your head, whenever you're moving your body around, do it slower, in half the time you do it right now.

Why? This directs the appeal of more intention in your actions and movements. People seek rapport with others who are intentional with their actions as often as possible because these people reveal a conviction of knowing what they want and where they'd like to be. That spells security: security in oneself, one's way of conducting themselves to others, and an overall security in their life.

Moving slower and speaking intentionally slower gives you more time to think about your exact actions and words with what you want to say. The more accurate and concise you can be with your actions and words, the more steadfast you appear to others.

You'll also feel more confident with yourself and what your own desires and beliefs are.

Moving and speaking slower also helps you to get the bottom of what your true desires are so that you can bring those into the world and share them with others.

As the saying goes, "Think fast and speak slowly".

#4 principle: be non-reactive.

Don't react to something outside of your reality. When you're talking with a girl and you hear a siren or a noise, do not turn your head. Stay focused on her and she will feel your masculine, dominant power. She won't look at the source of the noise and she will stay in the moment, following your high status behavior.

This principle speaks to others previously made in the book about being responsive over being reactive. Being reactive means that you just run with a feeling that was triggered within you. That, or jump into action or a train of thought without contemplating your next move, words, or the consequences that may or probably will arise from them in the bigger picture. Often being *reactive* in a situation can lead to further trouble or complications.

Being *responsive* means that you remain grounded in your central sense of conviction for yourself and your confidence. You may feel emotions triggered within you due to some situation, but you allow them to pass through you or channel them in some other way rather than get carried away by them in thought, verbal or physical reaction.

When you're responsive, you take your time to reply to a situation or stimulus mindfully and appropriately. You develop an ability to handle situations with ease, command, and a sense of humor.

Also, be aware of your fidgety movements and correct them: maybe you're touching your hands, or you're moving your feet as a sign of anxiety.

Stop doing that. Be still and relaxed.

#5 principle: lean back.

Learn to lean back most of the time.

Remember that leaning in is a really low status behavior. Learn to make people, especially girls, feel a subconscious urge to lean towards you, simply by leaning back.

This little trick will change the whole dynamic of your conversations, giving you the power of a badass.

This also means that when you're walking or just standing, you will have your shoulders up and back and your chin up. Just a masculine, healthy posture.

If you're talking to a girl in a loud club (or whatever loud place) then move slowly, lean in, whisper your words into her ear and then go back to leaning back. This will make her come to you whispering in your ear: that's how high status men communicate in loud places, without leaning in in a low status way.

If you want to know the other principles and the great exercises in order to train your Body Language, then search for Body Language Training on Amazon.com.

What if I told you that with some tips, your standing position could become a real sign of POWER?

What if after reading this short guide, you will be able to attract the girl you want, just sitting in a DOMINANT position or walking like a real badass?

Trust me, body language is really that powerful.

You should already know that human beings are constantly reading situations and other people so that, really quickly, they can know what category put them in: low status, middle status, and high status.

It's just a survival mechanism, because you have to know who has the power and who hasn't. That's something that's been hardwired into us over thousands and thousands of years.

So, most people don't trust words, because we've been taught from a young age to lie with them.

They prefer to read those status cues through the body language: THAT is the honest signal!

High status body language = high status person.

It's that simple, and we trust it.

Once we make the decision or opinion about that person, it's almost impossible for us to break it.

Therefore, your body language is the UNSPOKEN TRUTH.

When you have a high status body language, people conclude that you are in CONTROL of your own reality.

Remember this, my badass friend:

"The body follows the mind, but the mind follows the body even more."

Keeping a high status body language will make you have a high status mindset all the time: this can CHANGE YOUR LIFE for the rest of your days.

Now, this is what you'll discover in Body Language Training:

Why a High Status Body Language Is So Important For Your Life...

The 10 Foundational Principles of High Status Body Language...

My Best Tips and Tricks for Always Displaying a Powerful Body Language...

The Secret Badass Body Language Training...

What Your Walk REVEALS About You...

How To Make Sure She Finds Your Walk Sexually Attractive...

How To Get An Incredible Confidence In Your Walk...

...and much more!

Check out my other Training Books!

Voice Training: How To Unleash Your Inner Badass Vocal Power With Vocal Exercises, Become A Leader And Get A Deeper Voice In 7 Days Or Less

Voice is one of the most important qualities of a leader.

When you have a POWERFUL voice, life becomes so much easier. Your social life will be much better and your business life will reward you so many times. Girls will be much more attracted to you... and if you're a woman, your voice will be the SEXIEST it is ever been.

Just imagine yourself at a business meeting: you will be the most valuable guy there, because your voice will be so STRONG and COMMANDING.

Everyone will be raptured by your words.

Political leaders and actors were not born with a powerful voice, they TRAINED it up to that point.

In fact, you don't have a quiet voice, you simply trained it that way.

Now it's time to train it the other way around!

Here Is A Preview Of What You'll Learn In Voice Training...

Why A High-Status Voice Is So Powerful: how to make people know, like and trust you immediately...

The 5 Secret Traits Of A Powerful Voice: capture attention and hold it in a trance-like state every time you open your mouth!

Voice Training: mouth and voice strengthening exercises and tonality secrets used by Hollywood actors to command your audience's attention...

The Power Of Enunciation And Suspense: how to become a master storyteller who holds people rapt, fully engaged and hanging on your every word...

... and much more!

Eye Contact Training - How To Attract And Seduce A Woman, Increase Your Confidence And Become A Leader

What if I tell you that with some easy, powerful exercises you can get a deep, high status eye contact in just a few days? It would change your life, right?

Well, IT CHANGED MY LIFE. When you can handle the tension of a deep eye contact with everyone, you feel invincible. When you can handle the eyes of your boss, staring directly at them with confidence, then you'll stop feeling like his slave.

And with girls... damn, keeping a high status eye contact with girls it's completely GAME-CHANGING.

The techniques I show you in this book will make them chasing for your attention: they are so powerful, that even HOLLYWOOD ACTORS use them.

People will start doing things for you, they will start looking to you for decisions and, for the most part, they'll simply do whatever you say.

Remember this, my badass friend:

"With great eye contact comes great power, and with great power comes a lot of pussy."

Now, here is what you'll discover in Eye Contact Training:

Why a high status Eye Contact is so important for your life...

What a high status Eye Contact exactly is: one simple trick to deep, powerful, relaxed eye contact...

How to command complete control of your eyes and your attention: this SCREAMS high status to anybody watching...

Eye Contact Training: how to OWN your internal tension - Specific practices and exercises to train you how to handle tension inside and outside...

... and much more!

Confidence Training: - Become An Alpha Male by Mastering Your Confidence, Self Esteem & Charisma

Confidence is one of the most important traits to master if you want to succeed in your life.

While you decided to bet on yourself, most men out there are going to continue on their boring lives, controlled by their emotions, like weak little leaves in the wind. You will not.

You're meant for greatness, and I hope this guide will help you reach your goals and transform your life.

In fact, for some guys, mastering their emotions and becoming truly confident will be their graduation from little children to ALPHA MALES. Because from now on, your emotions will work for you, instead of the other way around.

I'm talking about pure, unshakable confidence, which means untouchable indifference and emotional mastery at its finest.

So you can finally start ENJOYING and LIVING LIFE like the king you know you are, staying cool, calm, and collected, no matter what life throws at you.

I'm talking about you finally being able to ask that girl out that you've so desperately wanted to.

I'm talking about you walking straight up to your boss' office and demanding that raise that you deserve (the right way) and getting it within the snap of a finger.

I'm talking about you finally being able to take on ANYTHING that life throws at you, without even flinching.

I'm talking about complete and utter state control over your emotions, for good.

I'm talking about laser-like focus, allowing you to get done in a day what most people get done in a month.

Let's get you going – you're ready for this!

Communication Skills Training: Learn To Powerfully Attract, Influence & Connect, by Improving Your Communication Skills

What can you do to train yourself into a badass speaker? How can you get the kind of responses you want from people?

With Communication Skills Training, you will learn to:

Spark a conversation and keep it **FLOWING** in any direction you want...

Build a heart-pounding emotional connection by triggering **DEEP** rapport...

Be completely **FREE, UNCHAINED** and **UNLEASHED** in your thoughts, words and actions!

Social Anxiety: Social Skills Training - Unleash Your Charisma! Overcome Anxiety, Shyness & Fear

In any and every kind of society structure... school... a job... a city...there are people who seem to have it all...

- The fame...

- The popularity...

- The recognition...

- The adoration and fawning...

Doors magically open for them in all kinds of life-changing ways.

It seems their life defies the laws of gravity. They're immune to failure.

While they're enjoying life to the fullest, you are spending your nights alone.

You know THE PAIN. The pain of being ignored.

And I know it too.

I used to be shy and reserved... just like you. And you know what?

One day I discovered that everyone can unleash their inner CHARISMA

so that they can start seducing not only girls, but the whole world, easily and naturally.

You have the inner power to break your "social anxiety cage" and free your true, awesome self.

You don't have to be creative. You don't have to fake anything...

Being charismatic is a skill that has immeasurable power and influence in the world.

Unleashing your charisma will help you overcome social anxiety, depression, shyness and fear.

You will soon be recognized as a valuable member of your social circle or, even better, as the leader.

After my Social Skills Training, you'll be able to land the best job opportunities, dream clients, major promotions and juiciest assignments. It's THAT easy.

After reading Social Anxiety - Social Skills Training, this is what will happen to you:

✓ People will instantly acknowledge you. They won't know quite why, but make no mistake, you're going to be a force to be reckoned with!

✓ You won't fear conversations with big groups of people - ever again!

✓ Doors will open. Opportunities, made especially for you, will present themselves. People will seek you out and remember you

✓ You will simply be the person in the room that everyone is drawn to!

Go get it now!

Made in the USA
Lexington, KY
21 May 2016